LECTURE NOTES
A DURATION POEM IN TWELVE PARTS

LECTURE NOTES
A DURATION POEM IN TWELVE PARTS

DEBORAH MEADOWS

BLAZEVOX[BOOKS]

Buffalo, New York

Lecture Notes: A duration poem in twelve parts
by Deborah Meadows

Printed in the United States of America

Interior design and typesetting by Geoffrey Gatza
Cover Art: Eva Hesse
Accession II, 1968 (1969)
Galvanized steel, vinyl
30 3/4 x 30 3/4 x 30 3/4 inches
Detroit Institute of Arts, Founders Society Purchase, Friends of Modern Art Fund, and Miscellaneous
Gifts Fund, 1979
© The Estate of Eva Hesse. Courtesy Hauser & Wirth
Photo courtesy Detroit Institute of Arts
Photo courtesy of Detroit Institute of Arts / Bridgeman Images

First Edition
ISBN: 978-1-60964-308-9
Library of Congress Control Number: 2018932944

BlazeVOX [books]
131 Euclid Ave
Kenmore, NY 14217
Editor@blazevox.org

publisher of weird little books

BlazeVOX [books]

blazevox.org

21 20 19 18 17 16 15 14 13 12 01 02 03 04 05 06 07 08 09 10

BlazeVOX

There is no reason to suppose, however, that the conceptual artist is out to bore the viewer. It is only the expectation of an emotional kick, to which one conditioned to expressionist art is accustomed, that would deter the viewer from perceiving this art.

— Sol LeWitt

Acknowledgments:

All segments of *Lecture Notes: A duration poem in twelve parts* are derived from notes I took during lectures part of the ongoing Cal Tech series open to the public. Mostly from the Humanities and Social Science Lectures, all occurred from March 14, 2007 to November 9, 2007 in Pasadena, California. My attendance was irregular and shaped by my teaching schedule and general availability. Part of my interest in "duration" is to explore how time may be more, or different, than "seat time" or "time served" on one's body, in one's thought, one's desire.

Lecture Notes: A duration poem in twelve parts may underscore how important yet flawed the handwritten process may be in contrast to, say, video or audio recording. All misspelling, abridgements of fact, inclusion of audience comment, and distractions from lecture are my fault for which I apologize. I refer readers to the works by those who gave the lectures; they are listed below.

Presently, there is no plan for this work to be taught at Cal Tech.

I refrained from commentary with the idea the reader would critically glean phrases such as "savagely attacked," "cooperate," "control," and the barely sub-surface (which by Lecture 5 is the overt topic) presence of the slave trade and its legacy driving the economies and thought-structures sustaining representations. Furthermore, I rely heavily on readers for critique and engaged reading of the ways that capital markets or human behavior are examined in projects, the background assumptions of virtue, worth, intention, the state of being informed, and how advanced scientific and other research may outstrip our current sets of vocabularies and representations and show those sets for the exhausted garments they are. How is it that art and science are so frail in the face of great power but uncannily durable?

Interleaved between each set of notes are excerpts from poets, artists, and thinkers such as Eva Hesse, Robert Smithson, Mierle Laderman Ukeles, Alain Badiou, Melvin B. Tolson whose works are what? guideposts? provocations? instigations? Time markers, flawed as they are, include daily news items from the day of the lecture and one item from a decade on.

Dedicated to Howie and all other Cal Tech alums

Listen Nods: A ration in twelve arts

... The machine? The grid? The cube? Repetition? Industrial processes? ... There is something more and other to be experienced about *Accession* than *any* of these words can account for, alone or in concert. The work concerns the senses and sparks desire with an immediacy that is anything but pregiven, and in ways that are not explained by a mere inventory of its materials or conceptual points of departure. The physical history of the three versions of the work offers its own record of those desires: when first shown, it was damaged by people climbing into it and had to be remade; to this day children are still lowered inside headfirst by indulgent parents and museum guards alike. Hesse herself was filmed bending over to stick her head inside and photographed with her hands poised within the bristling interior. ...

on Eva Hesse's *Accession* by Anne M. Wagner, "Another Hesse"

Method

The public is confronted here with the following art objects: eagles of all kinds, some of which are fraught with weighty symbolic and historical ideas. The character of this confrontation is determined by the negative inscription: "This is not … this is not a work of art." This means nothing other than: Public, how blind you are!

Thus, either-or: either information on so-called modern art has played an effective role, in which the eagle would inevitably become part of a method; or the inscription appears as mere nonsense — that is, it does not correspond to the level of discussion concerning, for example, the validity of the ideas of Duchamp and Magritte — and then the exhibition simply follows the classical principles: the eagle in art, in history, in ethnology, in folklore …

from "Method" section of catalogue of *Musée d'Art Moderne, Départment des Aigles* by Marcel Broodthaers

1. circularity of game, meta-strategies

Wednesday, March 14, 2007 lecture: "Conditional Commitments" by
Ehud Kalai

(Daily Note: *LA Times* reports on H & R Block's added sub-prime loan loss;
it's more than first reported)

(A decade later, March 14, 2017, *LA Times* reports: "Swastika, racial slur
carved into Orange Coast College security vehicles; ex-student held")

2. to square the circle (conform to canonic image) bear feeds itself

3. the experiment requires that you continue — you must go on

4. geodesic network

5. defeat/resist being turned into commodities

6. everyone is better off if we set up system
to protect minorities from majorities

7. see how to unstuck "Opportunity" ... which is
to put it in reverse & gun it

8. Found that: People do not befriend those
of similar ability (unlike academics ...

9. discrete actions not meaningful in themselves
that can be combined for meanings

10. no longer whether law of excluded middle is true
but one of choosing lang. wherein it is true or not

11. "committed types" stay in neighborhood

12. With telescope you can do some serious damage to cosmology

1. Lecture Notes

meta-strategies —

I cooperate if you cooperate
I won't cooperate if you don't cooperate

delegation game — on
computers get to read each
other before they decide

2 players

circularity — we condition
each other's action

both players choose
conditioning devices

device→strategy
similar to program equilibrium

*

— 2 players —
device chooses pure strategy

must device be   device must
sufficiently rich?   be voluntary
to play

----

        pricing game
2 vendors of TVs, their ads
in Friday newspaper

space of commitment devices

set — ads the newspaper allows
run

— prices generated in response
   to opponents' ads

strategy must be well-defined
yet is defined ["I will undercut
every opponent by 50"] by device

                    *

— commitment (or device) equilibrium
is an equilibrium (in mixed
strategies) of this game

Mixed strategies make a big difference
        [randomly selected device —
                matching pennies …]

prisoner's dilemma
        one-shot, tit-for-tat
        /   \
    cooperate   not-cooperate
                        aggressive

payoffs — like prisoner's dilemma

hunting with Cheney

                *

FL — coop. against FL but
(flexible   Agg. against
lawyer)   TLs

TL tough against all
tough lawyers

                              Nash equilibrium

→private-strategy (coop/agg)
        3rd and 4th

        private strategy not effective
at escaping circularity if game
is one of aggression-dominance

                    *

continuity of strategy
supposes alternating plays
f. may not be pure

correlated equil.→ common
                        knowledge

■   ■   ■

2/3   both
highest, but commitment device

                    *

Avant-garde art, which claims utter development, is infected by strains of maintenance ideas, maintenance activities, and maintenance materials. ... I am an artist. I am a woman. I am a wife. I am a mother. (Random order.) I do a hell of a lot of washing, cleaning, cooking, renewing, supporting, preserving, etc. Also, (up to now separately) I "do" Art. Now I will simply do these maintenance everyday things, and flush them up to consciousness, exhibit them, as Art.

from "Manifesto for Maintenance Art" by Mierle Laderman Ukeles

1. circularity of game, meta-strategies

2. to square the circle (conform to canonic image) bear feeds itself

Friday, March 30, 2007 lecture: "Visualizing the Mathematical Sciences in the Early Modern Period" by Volker Remmert

(Daily Note: Our labor union, California Faculty Association is getting closer to a settlement on our salary schedule and contracts. There have been no raises in four years; housing and gas are through the roof.)

(A decade later, March 30, 2017, *LA Times* reports: "Gov. Brown takes his transportation plan on the road, 'sanctuary state' bill amended")

3. the experiment requires that you continue — you must go on

4. geodesic network

5. defeat/resist being turned into commodities

6. everyone is better off if we set up system
to protect minorities from majorities

7. see how to unstuck "Opportunity" … which is
to put it in reverse & gun it

8. Found that: People do not befriend those
of similar ability (unlike academics …

9. discrete actions not meaningful in themselves
that can be combined for meanings

10. no longer whether law of excluded middle is true
but one of choosing lang. wherein it is true or not

11. "committed types" stay in neighborhood

12. With telescope you can do some serious damage to cosmology

2. Einstein Papers March

"wings" of arithmetic
& geometry

      <u>Primi mobilis</u> 1667
           <u>fabulae</u>
winged horse of geometry

Apollo & Pegasus
      linked, early mod.
          period

scholars & artists flying

not dangerous when
"right person riding
         Pegasus"

      *

     figures hold
tablets — personify
geometry & arithmetic

other representations more
difficult
     Three winged women
on frontispiece of Galileo   1655

geometry — arithmetic — optics

Mostly antiquity
means Greek antiquity
     but one Abrahamic example

      *

containing authority
by visual means

f r o n t i s p i e c e

*

Euclid's <u>Elements</u>

Archimedes ---------Euclid
                        the geometer

utility for military
"Archimedes at war"
yet cultural importance
of enduring value shown
by references from antiquity

        symbol of civilization
        — read shapes in
        sand at
        Rhodes

        *

1574
Copenhagen
speech
— astronomers
of past

         *

Urania, muse of astronomy
and iconographic figures

icon
engraved conforms to canon
image

              Harmonia
Amsterdam   Macrocosmica
                1661

— intense awareness
of visual aspects of astronomy

  Atlas ---- Hercules

Queen & Emperor of mathematics
& sub-disciplines such as
                ballistics

         *

                    Bettini's
beehive of mathematics

Apiaria universae
            philosophiae
            mathematicae
                    1645

[Aeolus ---- Neptune]

Aeolus smoking

(reference to god of winds
& tobacco trade in
Virginia)

math makes wealth

                    *

bears & roses
show bonds
of patronage,
            here.

                    *

for examples of patronage, Jesuits are
good examples — who
they had in mind, he produced
massive volume on sunspots
but then he died before
book was out so his brother
took it up

    <u>Rosa ursina</u>

        Scheiner, Christophe
        1626-30

(last 3 cantos of Dante
passages with sunspots,
blinded)
       the bear feeds itself

      *

pantograph,
to enlarge images

[impossible to
sq. the circle
with sledgehammer
or cannon]

                *

in tune with a gallery of popes

Last, from scientific debates,
esp. Copernican, yet less
prominent examples on
chronic sections
        found praise by Leibniz
4 methods to square the circle
made him laughing stock
      1647 — St. Vincent
(sun comes through
leaves as a circle)

               *

... The four lines of text, blind-stamped, with the exception of the conspicuously black periods, commas, acute and circumflex accents that seem to float randomly ... over the field, read as follows: "A form, a surface, a volume, subservient, an open angle, hard fishbones, a director, a female servant and a cashier. All day long, until the end of times.

from "Marcel Broodthaers: Allegories of the Avant-Garde" by Benjamin H.D. Buchloh, 1980

1. circularity of game, meta-strategies

2. to square the circle (conform to canonic image) bear feeds itself

3. the experiment requires that you continue — you must go on

Thursday, April 12, 2007 lecture: "Parietal-frontal Circuits for Decision Making" by Richard Andersen

(Daily Note: after this lecture when walking to my parked car, I overheard a CalTech student on his cell phone: "I can't fucking believe Vonnegut is dead." Death, or proliferation, of author?)

(A decade later, April 12, 2017, *LA Times* reports: "Calexit backers give up on ballot measure to secede, Feinstein faces tough crowd in San Francisco")

4. geodesic network

5. defeat/resist being turned into commodities

6. everyone is better off if we set up system
to protect minorities from majorities

7. see how to unstuck "Opportunity" ... which is
to put it in reverse & gun it

8. Found that: People do not befriend those
of similar ability (unlike academics ...

9. discrete actions not meaningful in themselves
that can be combined for meanings

10. no longer whether law of excluded middle is true
but one of choosing lang. wherein it is true or not

11. "committed types" stay in neighborhood

12. With telescope you can do some serious damage to cosmology

3. "Keep going, please"
"Until when?" "Until
it's necessary."
"The experiment requires
that you continue — you
must go on."
                    — on marker board

                *

Planning and decision-making
            in parietal-frontal
                        circuits

10 authors/co-researchers

— building brain-machine
            interface

cerebral cortex — higher functions
— movement-planning
phenomenon here —

1685 anatomical rendition
of brain shows it
undifferentiated

                *

abrupt change — Franz Gell
best known field of phrenology
                    1758-1828
studied criminals & prominent
people of his time — not sure
correlation there.

Broca — localization of function
one word, tan, defects
in speech

1991 Van Essen
— flattened sheet of folded
cortex, monkey
most areas we don't even know
            functional role
                    *

association — occipital
                    temporal
                    parietal

                    things are
dorsal path — where ^ in space
                    — also controls shifts
                        in visual attention

        1975
Mountcastle — monkey eye movement
            "command hypothesis"
quite a leap there

confusion partially semantic
but partly conceptual

saccades across room
            strong visual stimulus

                    *

from both fixation & saccade
cells had both
        movement & sensory
            responses

        between
bridge ^ motor & sensory

connections across wide areas
of cortex
        & across hemispheres

"think about a reach"
        "plan it"
            activates many areas
of cerebral cortex

I plan to move.

        *

monkeys & touch screen
             like ATM

monkeys like grad students
work in lab for 5 years, then
go to animal sanctuary
maybe grad students don't get that

attention — Wm. James
called it consciousness

we define it as high level
sensory plan.

        to separate attention
        from planning

           *

reach cells — saccade cells

de-coding a cluster,
simple trial, nearest neighbor

online control of reaching

    vision 90 milliseconds later

    proprioception 30 milliseconds

command signal
e.g., unfamiliar with plumbing in hotel,
cold water, turn, turn, turn,
still colder yet, then back to correct temp.

    *

do parietal neurons
encode past of future
movements?

obstacle — more use of past &
                    future
composite — reach activity
when target appeared
reach-region cells used
— show selectivity but
not for saccade choice

----------Reward set-up----------
— when monkey expects
orange juice instead of water,
more activity in cortex

                *

local field potential

spikes

field potential

gamma band oscillation, calculate
coherence, sinusoidal wave
      phase - zero   spikes
                            occurring
                            at peaks
                            of oscillation

does brain process information
using timing? ← very
              controversial

        *

coherence suggest bi-
directional communication
between areas — "choice"
gives more than "instructed"

search array onset

ideal observer — could you
tell which target the
monkey would choose?

subset of cells that coordinate
areas to solve problem
before plan is executed
            — so plans don't
            contradict each other

                    *

think about movement

is movement — prosthetic

can do this

another future direction

            virtual reality — track
eye movements

                    *

... I believe the whale got sick
That's why I have this Blues
I do believe one day,
He will finally turn me loose ...

"The Whale Has Swallowed Me," J. B. Lenoir, 1956

Estragon: Everything oozes.

from *Waiting for Godot,* Samuel Beckett

*

I'm thinking about how the first
                              ape-of-us
              first
              put together
        a box. ...

... I mean a box, man.
Four sides, 90 degree angles — the works.

from *First Box: A Poetics Theatre Play,* Rodrigo Toscano

1. circularity of game, meta-strategies

2. to square the circle (conform to canonic image) bear feeds itself

3. the experiment requires that you continue — you must go on

4. geodesic network

Friday, April 20, 2007 lecture: "Networks and Market Makers in the First Emerging Market: Bank of England Shares, London 1720" by Larry Neal

(Daily Note: On campus, noticeably heavy police presence after Virginia Tech shootings)

(A decade later, April 20, 2017, *LA Times* reports: "Trump sees cooperation from China in dealing with North Korean 'menace'")

5. defeat/resist being turned into commodities

6. everyone is better off if we set up system
to protect minorities from majorities

7. see how to unstuck "Opportunity" ... which is
to put it in reverse & gun it

8. Found that: People do not befriend those
of similar ability (unlike academics ...

9. discrete actions not meaningful in themselves
that can be combined for meanings

10. no longer whether law of excluded middle is true
but one of choosing lang. wherein it is true or not

11. "committed types" stay in neighborhood

12. With telescope you can do some serious damage to cosmology

4. Dissecting the Anatomy
of Exchange Alley:
The Dealings of Stockjobbers
in Bank of England
Stock during the South
Sea Bubble

1720
3 co-researchers

microstructures of stock
market gets codified
into rules & regs. beginning
19th cent.

        had been working
informally

            *

What accounts for success
of Britain's
                    Financial
Revolution?

lines of argument:

constitutional commitment
            (savagely attacked
                    by historians)
taxing power of parliament

                        1959
they go: with Peter Dixon's
        Chap. 17

— arm's length capital markets
encourage economic growth
            absorb shocks
            new tech.

                    *

How 1st market emerges?

— collapse of Mississippi,
        Dutch bubble,
        South Sea

availability liquid securities
        or customer base
        or microstructure?

Daniel
Defoe's def. of stockjobber

... wheedle, forgeries,
        falsehoods ...

Defoe's center of jobbing
                Cornhill

                        *

North of that

is commodities

bill of exchange

companies

                — Royal
                        Exchange

                *

London Coffee Shops

beginning
Jan 1698

        printed source
        of 3 days
        worth of prices

trades on Saturday

then rise
of "self-regulating
enterprise"

     unlike French
          case

    *

sociology of networks
"weakness of strong ties"

Data source includes
          Transfer Books 1720
                    ↓
          you find out what
trades go on, not just
prices, buyer/seller/
book value/date/amount
          of transfer

                    e.g., seller:
ledger no. Elizabeth Baker,
          spinster   buyer

                    *

embossed stamp
of 12 shillings per transfer

Robert Wesley
  a big trader & fills
pages & pages of ledgers

on other side
  bank acquisitions

South Sea bubble
  shows up even in
  Bank of England stock

    *

aftermath, people back
to paying average price

many 1-time buyers
but we selected for
15+ transfers, hence
jobbers

George Caswell   -

Robert Wesley   -

etc.

occupation
nobility
labor

variety of occupations
suggests not a tight
knit club

                    *

        1 woman jobber (widow)
married to naturalized
Dutch merchant
        — Johanna Cock —
[only after WWII women
allowed as directors of Bank
                of London]

                →for children
she places funds in trust
before collapse in South
Sea market
        shows she's smart

Women more likely
to deal with Caswell &
Wesley — they make
        up 10% of transfers

                        *

all are dealing with
large values in
stock

———————

    the sellers make out
better, get through
bubble

Wesley, Tohill, Gerhard

    geodesic network analysis

     *

Regression results

— people who trade
infrequently, deal with
market-maker guys

— people who trade
frequently, deal with
their own networks

      network of very
active dealer-jobber

        (bailout)
     government steps
in & doubles their
stockholding of S. Seas

       *

regular, reliable
annuities stabilizes South
Sea trade   — homogenous
          investments

contrast with Paris Bourse
       (closed down trading
         even at height of Miss.   much higher
moves it out of Paris — bubble   interest rate
            broken   for debt
no market-makers)

Amsterdam Beurs
       (kicked out &
       distributed all over,
       no price list around

has data on Dutch East
       India company (50%
          is Amsterdam)

         *

The Fifth Mirror Displacement:

At Palenque the lush jungle begins. The palisade, Stone Houses, Fortified Houses, Capital of the People of the Snake or City of Snakes are the names this region has been called. Writing about mirrors brings one into a groundless jungle where words buzz incessantly instead of insects. Here in the heat of reason (nobody knows what that is), one tends to remember and think in lumps. What really makes one listless is ill-founded enthusiasm, say the zeal for "pure color". If colors can be pure and innocent, can they not also be impure and guilty?

from Robert Smithson's "Incidents of Mirror-Travel in the Yucatan"

1. circularity of game, meta-strategies

2. to square the circle (conform to canonic image) bear feeds itself

3. the experiment requires that you continue — you must go on

4. geodesic network

5. defeat/resist being turned into commodities

Friday, April 27, 2007 lecture: "Acknowledging the Unthinkable: Returning the
Domestic Slave Trade to Its Central Role in the History of the United States"
by Steven Deyle

(Daily Note: Lingering talk of Imus firing and subsequent apology. How
genuine, etc.)

(A decade later, April 27, 2017, *LA Times* reports: "Pentagon is investigating
whether Trump's former national security advisor accepted improper foreign
payments")

6. everyone is better off if we set up system
to protect minorities from majorities

7. see how to unstuck "Opportunity" ... which is
to put it in reverse & gun it

8. Found that: People do not befriend those
of similar ability (unlike academics ...

9. discrete actions not meaningful in themselves
that can be combined for meanings

10. no longer whether law of excluded middle is true
but one of choosing lang. wherein it is true or not

11. "committed types" stay in neighborhood

12. With telescope you can do some serious damage to cosmology

5. Returning Domestic
Slave Trade to its Central
Role in Hist. of U.S.

       Carry Me Back
             Oxford 2005
      in addition to past
system of labor, an
investment device

buying & selling of
American-born slaves,
      not African

still dealing with impact
      on society

        *

frank if brutal depiction
of Am. past, some
might like to forget

Why we should not forget

_____

People ask him
why bring it up?
why not let people
forget?

not long ago that 1 group
of Americans owned another
group & didn't see
anything wrong with that

*

        some living children
of slaves
            many living grandchildren
of slaves

most incomprehensible system —
how could this be justified?

He thinks the slave trade
details tell us a lot

        abolitionist
Sturge ^ (1841) visited
Hope Slader — letter
"realize true nature of system"

                *

                    1790-1860
over 1 million forcibly
moved from Upper to Lower
South (Al, LA, Tx)
some moved with owners

boom in local slave trade
              Herbert
1975 Gutman — published
                              (1 sale every
frequency of sales   10 hrs)
slave was sold 1820-1860
every 3.6 minutes

Maybe more frequent
than Gutman & he
revised it upward

              *

             in last 30-40 yrs.
historiography has not
covered domestic slave trade
very much —

story of dom slave trade
is story of Am. society

colonial Am., 17th, 18th cent.
most arrived from Africa
or West Indies

After Am. Rev., slave trade
became indigenous operation

                  1 owner
       transferred from ^ to another

                  *

Closing (1808) Af. trade
increases domestic slave trade

                 ironic outgrowths
                   of Am. Rev.
hand-in-hand with Am. liberty

―――

changing attitudes toward
slave women

(took away from work time
but increase work force)

by late 18th cent. — perceptions
of women's ability to
reproduce as valuable
commodity — shows up in
sales advertisements

               *

by end of 18th cent.

reproductive ability
becomes part of appraised
value

changed view of enslaved
children (seen as
commodities & sold first)

— most sales are of children
moved from upper to
lower South
                    even 5 & under

                    *

economy of cotton

Chesapeake — transferred
"excess" slaves & helped fuel
southern expansion

increases in regional commitment
to chattel slavery — the trade
system made it more
profitable

always $200-300
more per slave in Louisiana
than in North

*

prices tripled

— Prime Male Hand —
        16
        18-25
healthy, strong
get most labor from
except skilled blacksmiths

in New Orleans — high end
                                price

1800   1860
$500. $1,800.

        today $30,000
        not a minor investment
        like luxury car today

                *

Hand Out

                    4 mill in 1860
                         slaves

$750. per person
total 3 billion dollars

most econ. historians
put it at $4 billion

3 times the capital
as in manufacturing,
in banks
7 times value of cotton
                              crop

48 times federal budget
_____

only real estate valued in NY

                    *

equity develops in slave
more important than
labor they produce

— use as collateral for
other investments

when Lincoln comes on
scene
threatened with loss
of "capital investment"
   80% of New Orleans'
loans secured with slave
& borrowing against them
    (makes it too valuable
      to give up)

   *

Abolitionist leaders
see public selling & evils
as

Disruption of Southern
family life — white & black

H. B. Stowe's book

                         Halley
if it were your ^ mother
about to
be sold   how fast could you
                              walk?

        notions of kind masters
are meaningless.

                 *

defend the indefensible

transfer property from one
        owner to other

South's largest form of wealth

yet nature of business
               offensive

generation of Northerners
now grew up without
having seen a sale —
       strongest opposition
             there

    *

                    in courts

        /   \

demand   denied that
we need   few sales
it   took place

paternalism — supposed
loving relation between
master & "his people"

        effective in defending
        slavery against
        Northern abolitionist

                *

intra-

scapegoat: slave trader
with all evils of system
that is otherwise a
fine system

the "imagined slave trader"
tore families apart
not planter

last chapter — effect
on enslaved. We all
need to remember
                devastating impact
                on their lives.

       *

Some fought back, ran
away, feigned illness at
time of sale.
        Efforts to keep families
together — if only in
memory — name new
child after one sold
away, continue to
tell stories of Virginia
family members

Frances Kimball, actress,
encountered woman with 9
children Tony fathers . . .

                *

. . . so many (her "husband"
sold away), so even though
9 children, Tony
not "real" husband.

      Slaves who could
send letters to family
sent through slave trader
               [letter e.g.
               "your loving wife
               Hannah Blair"]

defeat/resist being
turned into commodities

         *

murder cases
& torture

      South Carolina — white
men could only vote
for slaveholders (gov.
race, $10,000 & 100 slaves,
& lower for senate seat)

archive question — index
in LA on slavery

— unrecorded cases
Supreme Court

           *

— narrative, letters
filter through master

"people write things down
for a reason"

role of courts in slave trade
      (over 50% in M._____
initiated by courts — sheriff
himself got revenue)

           *

History is a book of seven seals
           from no Isle of Patmos;
but a Zulu Club Wit discovered
           it was a felony to teach
a black boy his ABC's when
           a whale ship was
                   the Harvard of
           a white cabin boy. . .

from *The Harlem Gallery*, Melvin B. Tolson

1. circularity of game, meta-strategies

2. to square the circle (conform to canonic image) bear feeds itself

3. the experiment requires that you continue — you must go on

4. geodesic network

5. defeat/resist being turned into commodities

6. everyone is better off if we set up system to protect minorities from majorities

Tuesday, May 15, 2007 lecture: "Comparative Judicial Politics" by Frances Rosenbluth

(Daily Note: on today's Yahoo page, "TV evangelist Rev Jerry Falwell dies at 73")

(A decade later, May 15, 2017, *LA Times* reports: "A Capitol gathering of Planned Parenthood supporters on Monday had many of the same traits as the January Women's March and other rallies of the Trump era: pink T-shirts and so-called pussy hats, with frequent jeers for the president and the GOP-majority Congress.")

7. see how to unstuck "Opportunity" ... which is
to put it in reverse & gun it

8. Found that: People do not befriend those
of similar ability (unlike academics ...

9. discrete actions not meaningful in themselves
that can be combined for meanings

10. no longer whether law of excluded middle is true
but one of choosing lang. wherein it is true or not

11. "committed types" stay in neighborhood

12. With telescope you can do some serious damage to cosmology

6. The Political Economy of
Patriarchy (not paper presented
but made)   Comparative
available)
Judicial Politics

("Today is Ditch Day —
shut the door")

          Explaining Court Behaviour

1) jurisprudential model
          problem — from standpt.
of politics
          *originalism
          (we ought to deduce
principles of law from Adam
                    Smith or anything)

          *

2) *attitudinal model —
there are types of judges
& presidential match, etc
then you know the outcome

3)Strategic model
*we might know types
but courts are in strategic
environment & going to
behave accordingly

          *

Judicial Independence
          — act independently
of political actors

          A. statutory review
          B. constitutional review

Normative reasons for
Judicial independence

— rule by law (higher
levels of confidence in outcome
& property rights)

          Think of China
trying to move to system
          of rules

                    *

— rule of law (is
set above politicians &
everybody has to
abide by) — everybody
is better off if we set
up system to protect
minorities from majorities

Why do courts behave as
they do — not as they
should

          — act independently of
legislators
          — how do you know
they don't in concert w/
                    politicians?

          *

— if one party going out
of power wants to hedge its
bets, it wants an independent
court to be arbiter between
it & gov.

                  Economists have
been testing
World Bank & IMF to
be Common Law vs.
Civil Law   ←←great Straw Man
                    to get World
                    Bank to do what
                    economists say

Common Law   r
                e   Shareholder
                la
                tion
                between ←protect against(?)
                        labor & other
                        interests

                *

political fragmentation
gives judges room for
maneuver
                — rules against
                easy re-composition
                of courts

                — life time tenure

can courts act against
short-term interest of
politician

                *

Latin Am. — presidents
sometimes have enough
resources to get legislative
majority such as Argentina
            whatever president
comes into power can bring
in his own court — new
expectation

            Founding Fathers —
don't worry about courts
doesn't have armies &
can't raise monies

                    *

When court may be
self-limiting if it thinks
it wouldn't have public
support.

Coalition governments
in parliamentary systems
operate according to
"treaties" that give
courts more or less room
for autonomy

        (Aside:
"Why was the woman
speaker scheduled for
Ditch Day?")

                    *

legis. & ex. branches
are fused in coalition gov.

          — they're in stronger
position to interfere with
judges' rulings

      depending on how
strong or fragile coalition

       empirical pattern
      when sig. diff
preferences | preferences
    of | of
  court | legislature

        *

7 periods of jurisprudential
       packages
↑ missing politics of why
          that
[Lockner - protecting   path
property rights]   is taken
           & not another

   - - - - - - - - - -

Puzzle of Minority Protection
majoritarian problem
in Westminster system
(politicians outnumber judges)

      — punish politicians who
step on their toes; it
could be their toes next day,
may be minority next time around

     *

But:

Factions roiling under
surface in UK system.

Questions — change like if
Iran gets nuclear weapon
— more a problem in parliamentary
system or not?

NOT SO UNIFIED
chancery courts, equity courts
                              in UK

state, federal courts in US
Can we endogenize rule
allowing dissent?
            Will they?
            They haven't taken
            a 2nd amendment case
            since 1937.

                    *

hierarchy or not?
supreme court   last
say? yet Supreme might
not take the case ...

            France — minority
leg. asks for judicial
ruling — throw sand
in wheel of legislative
majority
            very powerful right
of leg. minority but
weakens court's independence
by politicizing it.

                    *

How to measure
courts' independence?
                — how often court overturns

Mitterand tries to
nationalize industry,
courts said: sure
nationalize but can't
appropriate -- slowed
down because of cost

            cued to least
      /   substantive claims
U S — freedom of speech

in EU -- balanced
against damage of
hate speech

                *

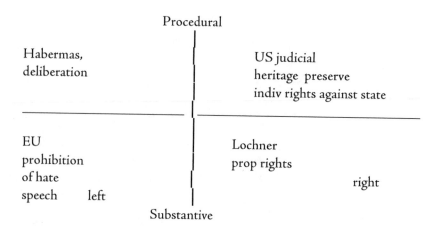

anarchists'
speech

FDR courts
retrenched over time

Procedural

Habermas,
deliberation

US judicial
heritage preserve
indiv rights against state

EU
prohibition
of hate
speech   left

Lochner
prop rights

                                    right

Substantive

— leftism substantive in
aims — not just equal
opportunity but aim for
equal outcomes

*

— Tocqueville
everyone in middle

— no-dissent rules
are endogenous

— coalition gov.t s
can be destabilized by
dissenting opinions that
injure the lives of
coalitional "treaties."

↑
those courts more likely
to agree on substance

*

pol. frag. gives space
for judicial autonomy

*

... by placing this picture on a heavy wooden tripod, Magritte does all that is necessary to reconstruct (either by the everlastingness of a work of art, or by the truth of a schoolroom demonstration) the site common to image and language. But this surface is also contested: for the pipe which Magritte had so carefully juxtaposed to the text, which he has enclosed along with the text inside the institutional rectangle of the painting or blackboard, has now escaped: it is up above, floating without references, leaving the text and the figure of which it should have been the link and the point of convergence on the horizon, only a tiny blank space, the narrow wake of its absence— as if it were merely the unparticularized mark of its escape. Then, on its beveled and so obviously unstable legs, the easel need only collapse, the frame break, the picture and the pipe roll on the floor, the letters scatter: the common ground — a banal work of art or an everyday demonstration — has disappeared.

from Michel Foucault's "Ceci n'est pas une pipe," translated by Richard Howard

1. circularity of game, meta-strategies

2. to square the circle (conform to canonic image) bear feeds itself

3. the experiment requires that you continue — you must go on

4. geodesic network

5. defeat/resist being turned into commodities

6. everyone is better off if we set up system
to protect minorities from majorities

7. see how to unstuck "Opportunity" ... which is to put it in reverse & gun it

Mon., July 9, 2007 lecture: "A Rover's Eye View of Mars" by
Steve Squyres and science team members NASA, Cornell University

(Daily Note: Notes on this exciting talk were particularly difficult to
write -- the seating area was darkened so we could take in the images sent to
NASA from Mars. During the talk there was mention that this week is a
national conference for the Mars results here in Pasadena, California. This
talk is not in the Humanities and Social Science Lectures series)

A decade later, July 9, 2017, *LA Times* reports: Fiction Bestsellers:
1. *The Handmaid's Tale* by Margaret Atwood ($15.95)
2. *All the Light We Cannot See* by Anthony Doerr ($17)
3. *Milk and Honey* by Rupi Kaur ($14.99)
4. *Commonwealth* by Ann Patchett ($16.99)
5. *1984* by George Orwell ($9.99)

8. Found that: People do not befriend those
of similar ability (unlike academics ...

9. discrete actions not meaningful in themselves
that can be combined for meanings

10. no longer whether law of excluded middle is true
but one of choosing lang. wherein it is true or not

11. "committed types" stay in neighborhood

12. With telescope you can do some serious damage to cosmology

7. "A Rover's Eye View of Mars"

Mars rovers launched
4 years ago

"Spirit" & "Opportunity"

Instead of being in
history books we are
perched on edge of
ingress of Victoria
Crater.

Steve Squyres — (about a
                        decade
                                on project)
Jim Bell — PI of camera

                    *

Dave Des Marais
                — ideas on geo-bio-
chemical cycle on Mars

Steve Squyres:

Mars 1250 days instead of "90-
day Mission" temp.
dry   desolate

valley less than
kilometer wide

                    *

dry riverbed —
                    It's a
hint that warmer & wetter
in past — layered
sedimentary rocks

(records conditions,
a forensic science

                    read story
                    rocks tell)

2 robot geologists

We experience Mars
through their sensors

                    *

infrared

spectrometer   &
periscope on mast

arm: shoulder,
          elbow & wrist are
in my exact dimensions,
Steve says, pure coincidence

RAT rock abrasion
          tool

_____

spacecraft — 3 petals
          folded up

                    *

encased in heat
shield, like Russian
dolls in dolls, . . .

Summer 2003
launch atop
2 delta rockets
at Mach 25 it hits
Mars' atmosphere;
at Mach 2 sends out
landing chutes

*

parachute blossomed
in Boise test
but failed

Solved with new design

Airbags — inflate
explosively, bounced
& rolled as much as
kilometer

*

once lands, petals

open up   origami
in reverse, turns itself

into rover.

solar panels must
unfold.

These can flip
themselves upside
down — ramp

*

rocker-boogie
suspension system

Steering,
endow vehicle
with vision, intelligence,
& decision-making
power — where to
go through path
of rocks

                    *

we can program
courage &
cowardice levels
            (driving)

RAT — diamond
tipped grinding tip

Lake basin &
dry rivers
basaltic rock

                    *

lava rocks
everywhere for
kilometers

2 1/2 kms away

Day 150 of 90-
day mission
found minerals
that had interacted with
            water
                    *

summit of Husband
Hill

1 wheel won't

turn so go backward

& drag front wheel

dumb luck uncovered
by drag mark:
90% pure
silicon dioxide
(opal) so we think
"hot springs"

                    *

solar   panels

        (350 watt hrs)

covered with
        dust
        down from 900-
                some watt
                        hrs.

One day gust,
lucky gust of wind
cleaned panels

                    *

major dust
storm in S. hemisphere
of Mars   — power
levels up

―――――――――――

                "Opportunity"

site selected

for chemistry

                hematite sometimes
                forms as consequence
                                of water

                    *

                                landed
in impact crater
(Tiger Woods could not
have sunk this shot)
saw "great wall"

very short
bounce-marks of
lander in this picture

―――――――――――

round things in
layered rock

we needed
gathering of blueberries
composition of

                    *

hematite

concretions

showing that <u>once</u>

at least, water

water once saturated

surface

— are there clues
of propagating ripples
of sand over sand

                    *

saw similar ripples
on Mars   — rarely
water flowed across
surface
Endurance Crater

          put together
"stratigraphic
          section"

We drove by
heat shield &
          its crater

                    *

we took

cross section images of
heat shield for
engineer (rarely do they
see their design after use)

Drove south
"bombing along at
top speed with our
eyes closed"

got all 6 wheels
stuck up to their hubcaps

                        *

1) play sand, 2) clay,
& 3) diatomaceous
earth is recipe
for Martian soil
so they could
see how to unstuck "Opportunity"

Spend 2 1/2 weeks
to find optimal
way to extract it

                        *

which is to
put it in reverse
            & gun it.

Magellan left
Spain with many,
ships and crew, & his 1 surviving
ship & 18 of 260
sailors so we
chose name
Victoria for crater
                        *

driving along
rim of crater &

imaging layers

of rocks

you'd believe

it is SW sandstone
                    Navajo.

———————————

list of at least
4,000 names at end of
his book of who
worked on Mars mission

                    *

Earth has Ansel
Adams, Mars
has Jim Bell:

red skies at day
becomes blue at
sunset on Mars,
reverse of Earth

material for a
future Mars poet

                    *

Phoebus & Demos
(from Sagittarius)
brightest things to see —

                    watch their
eclipse across

sun of Demos
& Phoebus

                 *

                      See

        Earth rise
        from Mars
        image

circumpolar
star trails at
night   — imaged
by cameras

                 *

volcanic sand

— black, no
quartz like in sand here on Earth
so all Mars' sand is like a black sand
beach in Hawaii but
not a palm tree anywhere

How frustrating to
not know time
to not be able to
do radio carbon
dating & not
know anything
about time
age of rocks

                 *

places named
after Magellan &
places his crew visited

Cape St. Mary

Cape Verde

Bottomless Bay

Cape of Good Hope

*

Cape Desire

— piece about
to cleave off

— putting together
sedimentary story

Golfo San Matias

*

Valley Without Peril

Cape St. Vincent

mosaic
Big dust storm
past week brewing . . .
blotting out
90% sunlight
dark & foreboding

started to dissipate

*

You can follow along
by going to:

http://marsrover.jpl.nasa.gov

http://pancan.astro.cornell.edu

get enough pictures
to wallpaper
your home with images from Mars

           *

Dave Des Marais:

Mars exploration
like building a
cathedral   — takes
many people
many years

Did life exist
on Mars?

           *

                life

       /   \

temperature   availability
                       of water

surface is
inhospitable

What about sub-
surface of Mars?

_____

Artist's representation
of what Earth may
have looked like 3 1/2

           *

104

billion years
ago   — we're
pretty sure surface
had life background
water there

Microbial
atmosphere Earth
single-celled life

                    *

Life

1) info storage
& replication

2) energy
harvesting &
transduction

3) organic
biosynthesis

We now know
our Earth's surface
biomass may be less
than sub-surface mass
microbial life
below our oceans
without sunlight

                    *

Thriving in
Darkness

oxygen   sulfur
iron   — can
react then life can
thrive without
sunlight

persistent
(near-surface

water   )

salty rich
like Yellowstone

use iron at
acidic springs —

              *

bio signatures

in rocks

              *

microbes in
areas & galleries
under Indian Ocean

they study them,

slowly digesting rock

we're learning more
about our own
biosphere beyond
study of
Mars

iron & sulfur
can be hydro-
thermal system

*

... The metonymic processes are reduction, expansion, and displacement, and these represent historical continuities and relations of experience in particular exempla. Closely related to, and taken as a kind of species of metonymy, is synecdoche, where the part is referred to by the whole, or the whole is referred to by the part, or something omitted is referred to by what is included.

[Jasper Johns'] *Untitled*, 1972 (Museum Ludwig, Cologne) (Fig. 8) is a painting of metonymic and synecdochic relations; it's an arrangement of fragments, bits of surfaces, cast parts of human bodies (male and female), traces of objects. Each pattern, object, imprint is there invoked by and to evoke other surfaces, authors, people and events defined by (even momentary) contiguities in time and place: painted and literary texts; painters and poets; sites seen while traveling in and around New York. Metonymy is what is represented and representing. ...

from Fred Orton's "On B#e#i#n#g# Bent 'Blue' (Second State): An Introduction to Jacques Derrida/A Footnote on Jasper Johns" in *Oxford Art Journal*, 1989

... The readymades themselves are not depicted. Instead the bicycle wheel, the hatrack, and a corkscrew, are projected onto the surface of the canvas through the fixing of cast shadows, signifying these objects by means of indexical traces. ...

from "Notes on the Index," Rosalind Kraus on Duchamp's *Tu m'*

1. circularity of game, meta-strategies

2. to square the circle (conform to canonic image) bear feeds itself

3. the experiment requires that you continue — you must go on

4. geodesic network

5. defeat/resist being turned into commodities

6. everyone is better off if we set up system
to protect minorities from majorities

7. see how to unstuck "Opportunity" ... which is
to put it in reverse & gun it

8. Found that: People do not befriend those of similar ability (unlike academics ...

Tuesday, September 25, 2007 lecture: "Social Incentives in the Workplace" by Iwan Barankay

(Daily Note: Driving home from CalTech today, I heard on NPR coverage of the 50th anniversary of the "Little Rock Nine" who integrated Little Rock's Central high school. One speaker called for students present today to "never forget from whence they come.")

(A decade later, September 25, 2017, LA Times reports: "Cowboys kneel before national anthem on Monday Night Football")

9. discrete actions not meaningful in themselves
that can be combined for meanings

10. no longer whether law of excluded middle is true
but one of choosing lang. wherein it is true or not

11. "committed types" stay in neighborhood

12. With telescope you can do some serious damage to cosmology

8. Social Incentives in
the Workplace (joint researchers)

field experiment in company
            they wanted tenure, bonus-
schemes, etc. but

how people respond to
contracts & people they
work alongside

— social relations shape
incentives & constraints
— in labor market, social
ties have key role

ties — friendship links

                    *

test whether & how
presence & identity of
worker's friends affects
her performance

These results we are
confident about (maybe
over a glass of wine
I'll tell about those
I'm less confident about)

            — positive, role models
contagious enthusiasm
            — neg. bad apples
contagious malaise

                    *

data   — firm's records on
productivity, our own
survey on social ties

farm   — organic produce
British strawberries
focus on fruit picking tasks

20-25 students
of Eastern Europe get
jobs, stay in caravans,
stay short period
of time

observe pickers with friends
& other days without
friends present, then

compare productivity

> *

paid by piece rate
(by kilogram) so not
related to productivity
of coworkers

UK farm, 2004
all live & work
on site

pick fruit principally

each day, supervisor gives
each person one row
to pick (no other
tasks such as carrying)

strawberries grow on ground
            2 hectares average field

> *

piece rate is announced
every day

— productivity in kilograms
            picked per hour

— bar code to identify
            worker

Asked workers to fill
out survey in 7 languages
& name 7 friends
2 or 3 weeks after arrival

Question: How many
workers? 1,000 over
season, they come & go
as classes begin

                        *

If you ever do this,
people very willing
to report on friends

Variation
            — type & quantity of
food that can be picked

Supermarkets call up with
food orders, so workers
sent to pick that particular food

— pick with friends
& workers are more productive

                        *

— if previous day w/friends
makes picker tired
from working harder,
       so varied those

          Found that:
People do not befriend
those of similar ability
(unlike academics where we
are of similar ability)

          Does
field productivity vary
as share of pickers
who are "connected"
       vs. "isolated" i.e.,
not with friends

       Supervisors & workers
put people together when
field day shock occurs

          *

cost

no homogeneous effect —
— not all workers
        work harder in presence
        of friends

— people work differently
        with friends

        heterogeneous effects
— formula for social
incentive on individual
workers

effect is positive for 2/3 workers
negative of 1/3 workers
        — possible some work
harder, less hard on

                    *

individual ability
        fixed effect to
construct distribution
        of ability on farm

            bottom quartile speed
            up 30% when
            moved in presence
            of friends

what behavior models
underpin results

people seem to derive
utility from being with
others

Is it function of how long
at farm?

                    *

                    Ques.
do some slow down
on row to complete
conversation?

          Don't think this
is chit-chat issue

if you ignore social
contexts when placing
people, you are losing
an important insight
on productivity &
friendship

                    *

Price of Conformism

— if workers motivated
by monetary & social
incentives

1) if a lot of fruit, a worker
is not willing to
slow down if there
is a friend

2) workers change behavior
to conform with friends

A few very good pickers
can lift up weaker
pickers
          10% increase

                    *

differs from Mass' study
of cashiers

workers will sacrifice
earnings for friends

what if we give workers
power to choose who
to work with

In 2005, we let
them be in teams of 5
       — introduced performance
       ranking
       — then introduced
       a prize competition

       good
workers tend to conform

       *

Question: But what if
fast pickers given
a more fruit-heavy
row are slowed but
still in communication
with others through
work-songs?

Ans.: I heard no songs.

Q.: And given the
many languages, the
shared song would
be The Internationale?

       *

... Nothing should be altered in this area. Scattered wood and earth shoring should remain in place. Everything in the shed is part of the art and should not be removed. The entire work of art is subject to weathering and should be considered part of the work. The value of this work is $10,000. The work should be considered permanent and maintained by the Art Dept. according to the above specifications.

from instructions on how to maintain *Partially Buried Woodshed* by Robert Smithson upon donation to Kent State University

1. circularity of game, meta-strategies

2. to square the circle (conform to canonic image) bear feeds itself

3. the experiment requires that you continue — you must go on

4. geodesic network

5. defeat/resist being turned into commodities

6. everyone is better off if we set up system
to protect minorities from majorities

7. see how to unstuck "Opportunity" ... which is
to put it in reverse & gun it

8. Found that: People do not befriend those
of similar ability (unlike academics ...

9. discrete actions not meaningful in themselves that can be combined for meanings

Tuesday, October 2, 2007 lecture: "Evolving a moral faculty: domain-specificity, neural specialization, and universality" by Marc D. Hauser

(Daily Note: In today's news, LA workers get deal on contract -- six unions represent about half of city workers. Ends chance of threatened municipal strike.)

(A decade later, October 2, 2017, *LA Times* reports: "Gov. Jerry Brown, lawmakers say they 'stand with the people of Nevada' after mass shooting")

10. no longer whether law of excluded middle is true
but one of choosing lang. wherein it is true or not

11. "committed types" stay in neighborhood

12. With telescope you can do some serious damage to cosmology

9. Evolving a moral
faculty

Moral "lemons" from
childhood to aboriginals

my daughter
when I asked "Who's the
man?" she learned
to say "Charles Darwin"
                    she gave
moral dilemma:
            5 people in cave, 1 entrance
woman wants ticket, too
big, gets stuck
            what do you do?
            blow her up?

                    *

BBC news:
            stuck woman traps
            SA cave group

            ↑
            South African

— Language & morality —
— Moral domain — how
            does your brain know
it's in it?
— moral domain, neural data
— unwind principles &
how does culture
change or shape

                    *

Lang. — mind-internal
conceptual system
designed for thought &
externalized

        Broad
Faculty of Lang. —
— true - if memory damaged
      so too lang, but
      memory does things
      unrelated to lang.

          Narrow — unique
to humans & to language

      *

syntax/semantics/phonology

Chomsky   —   Rawls
     /   \
how he   think about
framed some   source of moral judgments
questions   is a faculty
                comprised of
                abstract
                principles
                without specific
                content

Principle — impermissible
        to use a person to
        a greater good
no example of who or what
                particulars

                    *

Morality — designed
for intuitive judgments

        how we judge

   ‹

        what we do

phonemes   "actemes"
     /   \
     /   discrete actions
     /   not meaningful
     /   in themselves
     /   that can be
     /   combined for
     /   meanings
     /   \
grammatical   ethical
judgment   judgment

            *

                                            125

both have dedicated
circuitry

some inaccessible conscious
          awareness & immune
          to cultural influence

Thus far:
Kohlberg, Kantian view

Humeian — largely
driven by emotions

36 mo., 200,000 subjects
logged on   120 countries
13-70 yrs. to
answer variety of
moral & nonmoral questions

                    *

flip switch to kill
heavy man on tracks
before saving 5 people

               harm as intended
               means to greater good

but case with weight
on track — harm as not
method, intention

— obligatory —

Aquinas (law, Cath. church)

— Doctrine of Double Effect

intended harm worse
than . . .
Action — harm caused
by action is morally
worse than than omission
               *

126

Most people say actions
worse than omissions

is there a specific
rule innately in
humans (killing is
worse than letting die)

actions are more transparent
form of causal
responsibility

Method to what degree
            —cause
            —intended the outcome
            —morally worse

                        *

Do animals have building
blocks of certain kinds
of moral destruction?
                        Is it all consequences?
Do means matter?

Tamarins, Rhesus, Chimpanzees

task show 2 empty cups,
food placed in cup behind screen
            screener touches cup &
                        they touch it
2nd screener flops hand on cup

Nature of cooperation — do
animals care more about
consequences/rewards or
the means?

                        *

work with Damasio et
al   — emotions tell us
about moral domain
or not?

frontal lobe damage cases
          — measure social
emotions — a flattening,
emotions not causally necessary

more likely to say yes
in personal dilemmas,
utilitarian results such
as pushing fat man on track

                    *

Religion
          beliefs / outcomes

Law
          intentions

attempted harm

unknowing harm

                    anterior
                    cingulate

ventromedial cortex

no diff. of atheists & religious

Chiapas case — exception
          to pattern

                    *

                    (a guy using
virtual reality to
repeat Milgren experiments)

          shows recursive
device in lang., music, etc.
may be expressive of lang.
or no relation to lang.
though lang. uses it . . .

          *

... It is important to note how many 'books' of philosophy are in fact lecture notes, either kept by the lecturer himself and subsequently published (this is the case for a major portion of Heidegger's work, but also for figures like Jules Lagneau, Merleau-Ponty and others), or taken by students (this is the case for almost all the works by Aristotle that have been handed down to us, but also for important parts of Hegel's work, such as his aesthetics and his history of philosophy)....

In other words, it is impossible to provide a clear-cut criterion for what counts as a book of philosophy. Consider then the case of these *Theoretical Writings*: in what sense can this present book really be said to be one of my books? ... Is it not rather a book by my friends Ray Brassier and Alberto Toscano? After all, they gathered and selected the texts from several books, ...

... I would like to thank them because they have provided me, along with other readers, with the opportunity of reading a new, previously unpublished book, apparently authored by someone called 'Alain Badiou' — who is reputed to be none other than myself...

from "Author's Preface" to *Theoretical Writings* by Alain Badiou, edited and translated by Ray Brassier and Alberto Toscano

1. circularity of game, meta-strategies

2. to square the circle (conform to canonic image) bear feeds itself

3. the experiment requires that you continue — you must go on

4. geodesic network

5. defeat/resist being turned into commodities

6. everyone is better off if we set up system
to protect minorities from majorities

7. see how to unstuck "Opportunity" ... which is
to put it in reverse & gun it

8. Found that: People do not befriend those
of similar ability (unlike academics ...

9. discrete actions not meaningful in themselves
that can be combined for meanings

10. no longer whether law of excluded middle is true but one of choosing lang. wherein it is true or not

Wednesday, October 10, 2007 lecture: "Two Concepts of Scientific Philosophy: Carnap and Reichenbach" by Andre Carus

(Daily Note: In today's news is how "The U.S. State Dept. may phase out use of Blackwater private security guards in Iraq after review revealed Blackwater guards protecting U.S. Embassy convoy in Baghdad are accused of killing 17 civilians.")

(A decade later, October 10, 2017, *LA Times* reports: "Sonoma County officials on wildfires: 'This is nowhere near over'")

11. "committed types" stay in neighborhood

12. With telescope you can do some serious damage to cosmology

10. Two Concepts of Scientific
Philosophy — Carnap &
Reichenbach

Intro of Reichenbach's
widow, Carnap's
daughter & granddaughter
          ↓
came here from Stuttgart
at 12 in 1965 — she
said, after Stuttgart, it
was heaven

Reichenbach's <u>Lecture</u>
<u>Notes on Einstein's</u>
<u>Relativity Lectures</u> are
held here & at Pittsburgh

                    *

Today's speaker's dissertation
on why there was not
Enlightenment in Germany
          (Cambridge)

scientific philosophy

where to draw line between
geometrical reasoning &
other aspects of life

mathematicians used since
antiquity (Euclid
can't be accounted for
by Aristotelian logic

Gottlieb, Russell, Frege
early Wittgenstein
what

                    *

logical empiricists
take over most phil.
depts.

60s on, idea of scientific
phil. in doghouse

sub-group complicates
log. empiricism
      Hilbert, Einstein
is seen & appreciated
for heterogeneity & contributions

main figures Carnap
& Reichenbach
      — what did they have
in common

*

1923 first met, friendship
constituted logical empiricism

Carnap (utopian?) &
R. (as deflationist)?

Carnap saw Enlightenment
needed overhaul
        — did he succeed?

C.:
<u>ideal of explication</u>

background — both in
      front, active in
socialist movements, in
Germ Youth movement
enthusiastic but Einstein
physics, both studied physics

*

Reichenbach — prescient
in criticizing things
tending toward militarism
Romantic mumbo jumbo
in Youth movement

Carnap — saw creative
nonconformity in Youth
movement

hence divide between 2

both active in left wing
& socialist groups, student
groups

                    *

Carnap's logical construction
of world, axiomatic
space-time study

struggle of forces?
imagination (keep people
intermediated & conform
to power) unlike critical
intellect

Carnap
numbers & non-spatial
things, so imagination
created God, outside
space & time —
            all encompassing
space, how can I get
there from here? i.e.,
from my own immediate
experience

                    *

genuine knowledge vs. fake
(descended from tradition, etc.)

Newton (encyclopedists) —
gold standard

With abstract portrayal
up to logicism,
down to experience
undermined by Hilbert

Tarsky

all true sentences of math
as provable

Reichenbach — we know
nothing with certainty
we need to make best of
our uncertainty

*

& reject 2-value (true/false)
logic, replacement process

evidence doesn't determine lang.
he says doesn't matter

similar to Quine

C. — meta-language, but
he gave this up & went
to plural-languages

state principles, not words
changes conceptual disputes
— no longer seen as having
an answer, but a choice
of language. No longer
abstract objects or concrete particulars
but matter of choosing lang.

*

no longer whether law
of excluded middle is true
          but one of choosing
lang. wherein it is
true or not

relation of ordinary &
various scientific languages
becomes dialectical
which candidate explanations
are preferable
              & also in
background of extra-scientific
ramifications (social,
economic, etc.) so all
our values are brought
to bear.

                    *

Science (true has human
values) but has role
of predicting future
          so predictability matters

                    R. —
surplus meaning could
assign higher value to
realistic rather than
phenomenalistic, etc.

Doesn't matter … much
does this table exist? is
a matter of language
we choose to operate
within

              *

Reichenbach: in mainstream of
Enlightenment, better
knowledge sought, impersonal
higher probability

Carnap: doesn't require
impersonal (volitional elements
included, values, etc.)
          choice of lang. mattered
can have impact on
implications & applicability
of friendship in science

What is genuine reasoning?

                    *

precise scientific procedure
              and
vague ordinary language
      associative

Enlightenment tradition
one is reduced to other
(reductionist)   late
Carnap mediates between
extremes, he sees place
for both

Two like 2 great Germ. novelists:
Carnap, like Musil — heroic fragment
soaring ambition &
admirable
                  CC. — fragmented
                          work
T. Mann — finished oeuvre
(like R. trajectory & unity
of problems, lifelong)

                    *

— some like Rorty, anti-Enlightenment
          this is all behind us

— others find in present
circumstances find this
still important

famous tension: R. hostile
          to Popper
          Carnap hostile to
Quine

Carnap — question on
extension of Hilbert's
program

                    *

R.'s widow: memories of Einstein,
she knew Carnap,   " , etc.

She says: Hans was one of 5 people
in Einstein's first
class, they would all
take transportation together,
continue to discuss

          : Hans' first book, she
translated, and T. of Rel.
Hans gave galleys
to Einstein who made
marks. She has this book
          2nd book:
Phil. of Space & Time

In Princeton they always
saw Einstein & N. Bohr
there

                    *

another story: Ein. said Bohr talks
too much or doesn't listen

Ein. always wanted to
talk about quantum physics

end of widow's stories, and
"Mrs. Reichenbach is 98."

                        *

doves exist, dreamers, and dolls;
killers exist, and doves, and doves;
haze, dioxin, and days; days
exist, days and death; and poems
exist; poems, days, death

from *Alphabet* by Inger Christensen, translated by Susanna Nied

1. circularity of game, meta-strategies

2. to square the circle (conform to canonic image) bear feeds itself

3. the experiment requires that you continue — you must go on

4. geodesic network

5. defeat/resist being turned into commodities

6. everyone is better off if we set up system
to protect minorities from majorities

7. see how to unstuck "Opportunity" ... which is
to put it in reverse & gun it

8. Found that: People do not befriend those
of similar ability (unlike academics ...

9. discrete actions not meaningful in themselves
that can be combined for meanings

10. no longer whether law of excluded middle is true
but one of choosing lang. wherein it is true or not

11. "committed types" stay in neighborhood

11(A). Tuesday, October 16, 2007 lecture: by Vicente Fox "Revolution of Hope: The Life, Faith and Dreams of a Mexican President"

(Daily Note: Today "Putin warns U.S. against attacking Iran" and "Vice President Dick Cheney and Democratic presidential candidate Barack Obama are distant cousins.")

(A decade later, October 16, 2017, *LA Times* reports: "The African American Film Critics Assn. proclaimed 2017 the "Year of the Woman in Cinema," in a statement Monday announcing the honorees for its ninth annual awards ceremony.")

11(B). Monday, October 22, 2007 lecture: "Schelling Redux: An Evolutionary Dynamic Model of Residential Segregation" by William H. Sandholm

(Daily Note: Southern California wildfires are zero percent contained)

12. With telescope you can do some serious damage to cosmology

11(A). This is the flier for the Vicente Fox talk. When Howie and I arrived, the line wrapped around the buildings in front of Beckman auditorium, so we were unable to attend due to limited seating. Howie mentioned that Vroman's, our local independent bookstore, was a co-sponsor, and I remarked on how much they do for authors.

Vicente Fox: *Revolution of Hope*
The Life, Faith and Dreams of a Mexican President

Tuesday, October 16, 2007 at 8:00 PM
Beckman Auditorium
FREE; no tickets or reservations required

The former president of Mexico will read from and sign his new book.

When Vicente Fox swept into office in 2000, he broke the dictatorial one-party rule that had strangled Mexico for over seventy years. A native son of Mexico, grandson of immigrants from the United States and Spain, Fox worked his way from ranch hand and truck driver to the youngest CEO in the history of Coca-Cola. His political rise from precinct worker to world leader was equally swift. As president, Vicente Fox steered Mexico's fragile young democracy through turbulent times, ushering in six years of economic stability and reform in health care, education, and housing, with increased freedom of the press. His presidency also reduced poverty and tackled corruption.

In *Revolution of Hope*, President Fox outlines a new vision of hope for the future of the Americas. He speaks out forcefully on global topics such as immigration, the war in Iraq, racism, globalization, the role of the United Nations, free trade, religion, gender equity, indigenous rights and the moral imperative to heal the global divide between rich and poor nations, and reveals for the first time the ups and downs of his close but rocky relationships with world leaders from President George W. Bush and Prime Minister Tony Blair to Fidel Castro, Vladimir Putin and Hugo Chávez.

From the man who brought true democracy to Mexico, *Revolution of Hope* is a personal story of triumph and a political vision for the future.

This event is co-sponsored by Vroman's Bookstore.

11(B). An Evolutionary Dynamic
Model of Residential Segregation

Although racial segregation
has been easing since 70s
        it persists
        in most cities

Schelling (1971) "Dynamic
Models of Segregation"

his 2 models
        — spacial proximity
                agents think of
        moving to another location

        — isolated neighborhood
model — agents choose
between mixed or homogeneous

*

Schelling interested in
disequilibrium dynamics
           Will integrated
neighborhoods fall apart?
           "neighborhood tipping"

formal model of dynamics
of segregation without
Schelling's sorting
assumptions

           2-dimensional
           how many blacks?
           how many whites?

not true for general game
dynamics, this moves
toward equilibrium

                    *

Schelling — one bounded
area, black or white,
each lives there
unless color exceeds
some limit (tolerance)

population masses

| | m_w | whites |
| | m_b | blacks |

| θ_w | θ_b | tolerance |
| | | levels |

μ_w , μ_b

tolerance
levels

$(x_w$, $x_b)$ social state, masses
for each group

*

assumption — at any
        one time the agents
        in neighborhood are the
        ones whose tolerance
        are the highest

2 to 1 whites to blacks —
then who wants to
enter neighborhood or leave?
        Schelling
        " ... people leave in
the order of their discontent
leaving those most tolerant"

there is a segregated
                  equilibrium

        *

Bayesian population
                    game

how many whites
type theta p
              & set of strategies
set of strat. distributions

           current aggregate
                       behaviour
to best responses

           $B_P(x)$

              direction of
is moving in ^   sub-population's
best response

                              *

"committed types" stay
in neighborhood

proportion of blacks
　　　　choosing <u>in</u>

social state　　　　　　　aggregate equilibrium

mass of whites who are <u>in</u> = mass
who find it optimal to be <u>in</u>

　　　　　　*

Can we use a
similar trick to study
dynamics?

aggregate solutions
checking stability results
(over type by type)

could be a 50-50
split & some people
leaving & replaced
by same, moving
toward integrated
equilibrium, could be
moving toward
segregated equilibrium   stable
           all-white   asymptotically^
           all-black   "   stable

                *

```
        sink      vs.      saddle
          /                   \
integrated              inequality
equilibrium

let's suppose only
black agents are indifferent
  some white agents leave,
number of white agents
are back
            on the other hand
by kicking out some white
agents, white-black
ratio more in favor
of blacks, so more
blacks will want in


        before equil. is restored

                *
```

small disturbances
get magnified

    & we move away
    from equil.

in few games, does
convergence occur
         but
in our example
    competitive differential equation
        white/black

increase # of blacks,   down
  entry level of whites goes ^

& visa versa

       *

Extensions
— what if used taxes
  to promote integration

— many prefer integrated
  neighborhoods

How to extend to
  segregation by income
seg. by preferences for
            public goods

We'll have four
dimensions, etc.

                    *

... Waves of information are continuous, but their visibility is reliant on exposure. The blinking signals that illuminate Pierre Huyghe's works — from *L'Ellipse* to *No Ghost Just a Shell* to *A Journey That Wasn't* — are indicative of shifts in space-time relations that can be perceived only through the alternation of time codes. ... If structures can be folded they can also be unfolded and, most significantly, it is only once the creases of the past return to visibility that a new form might emerge.

from *Parallel Presents: The Art of Pierre Huyghe* by Amelia Barikin

1. circularity of game, meta-strategies

2. to square the circle (conform to canonic image) bear feeds itself

3. the experiment requires that you continue — you must go on

4. geodesic network

5. defeat/resist being turned into commodities

6. everyone is better off if we set up system
to protect minorities from majorities

7. see how to unstuck "Opportunity" ... which is
to put it in reverse & gun it

8. Found that: People do not befriend those
of similar ability (unlike academics ...

9. discrete actions not meaningful in themselves
that can be combined for meanings

10. no longer whether law of excluded middle is true
but one of choosing lang. wherein it is true or not

11. "committed types" stay in neighborhood

12. With telescope you can do some serious damage to cosmology

Friday, November 9, 2007 lecture: "The Specter of the Telescope: Radical Instrumentalism from Galileo to Hooke" by Ofer Gal

(Daily Note: On Spanish-language TV: "Elecciones Controversiales en Bogota, Columbia" The signs read: "se robaron de las elecionnes de los negros" that are held at the candidate's bedside.)

November 10, 2007
(Daily Note: Norman Mailer died.)

(A decade later, November 9, 2017, LA Times reports: Hillary Clinton helps Seth Meyers with some jokes he can't tell: "According to a recent article, Chardonnay is making a comeback," Meyers noted.
"And they said I wouldn't be able to create jobs," quipped Clinton.)

12. Specter of the Telescope

Galileo to Hooke

The wig & the lens

Hooke's presentation
of inverse Square Law

15 yrs before he
started corresponding
with Newton

he thought he was
taking this from Kepler

        *

perspectivist tradition
            — he takes his optics

— how to think
about decline of light?

1) mathematize light
2) physicalize optics

The Comet of 1577

optics was about
visual rays

        — they allow
ontology, us to see

       *

no one thought
they were same as light

observation with instruments
w/new, higher claims
& expectations

              lack of parallax
              they are in heaven

"light, are not only
poured upon but are
also imprinted ..."
               — Kepler
      1604

          *

findings they apply —
— light does not diminish
with distance

— light "same" everywhere

— human eye –pupil,
     a window
           (there is nothing
inherently wrong in
using an instrument)

— it takes intellect to correct
physical reception —
turns upside down
on return

     Where does intellect
get its stuff to correct
eye?

       *

camera obscura strives
to un-mediate vision

vision as "it really
is" before mediation
by intellect

big guy next to small woman
　　　　even though they
　　　　sit 30 cms. apart
　　　　in painting

————————

With telescope you can
do some serious
damage to cosmology

　　　　　　*

The Assayer Galileo
defend against
dinosaurs of church
who refuse to look
through telescope

is embarrassingly
reactionary — still has
Aristotelian ideas

— argues against
parallax by having
old fashioned view of comets

　　　　　*

Comets of 1618

Grassi's <u>Disputation</u>
       comet beyond moon &
       we, Jesuits are
anti-Aristotelian
— Galileo writes in 1623
to unmask Grassi
or Cassi … etc.

      not sublunar
      but celestial

        — our comet

Jesuits more forward
in their science than
supposedly "revolutionary" Galileo

       *

2 Jesuit claims Galileo opposes

1) telescope's magnification
depends on distance

2) no parallax of comet
can also be seen with
naked eye & eye always —
that's credence over use
of instrument.

Galileo argues "eye mediates
& introduces error
2) telescope goes through
artificial to natural
      telescope not like
spectacles to improve
sight but gets directly to nature
— telescope always magnifies
<u>strictly a mathematical relation</u>

*

                    telescope
allows reason to
bypass eye & read
mathematical figures

Hooke — instruments do
their own thing

            add more instruments
            & more

— that people didn't want
to look through telescope
is propaganda

                    *

The Lecturers:

1. Wednesday, March 14, 2007
Bray Theory Workshop
4:00 pm, 25 Baxter
Conditional Commitments
Ehud Kalai
James J. O'Connor Distinguished Professor of Decision and Game Sciences and
Professor of Mathematics
MEDS, Northwestern University

(Daily Note: *LA Times* reports on H & R Block's added sub-prime loan loss;
it's more than first reported)

(A decade later, March 14, 2017, *LA Times* reports: "Swastika, racial slur
carved into Orange Coast College security vehicles; ex-student held")

2.Friday, March 30, 2007
Seminar on History and Philosophy of Science (HPS)
4:00 pm, Einstein Papers Project, 363 S. Hill Ave.
Visualizing the Mathematical Sciences in the Early Modern Period
Volker Remmert
University of Mainz

(Daily Note: Our labor union, California Faculty Association is getting
closer to a settlement on our salary schedule and contracts. There have been
no raises in four years; housing and gas are through the roof.)

(A decade later, March 30, 2017, *LA Times* reports: "Gov. Brown takes his
transportation plan on the road, 'sanctuary state' bill amended")

3. Thursday, April 12, 2007
Brain, Mind and Society Seminar
4:00 pm, 25 Baxter
Parietal-frontal Circuits for Decision Making
Richard Andersen
James G. Boswell Professor of Neuroscience
Caltech

(Daily Note: after this lecture when walking to my parked car, I overheard a
CalTech student on his cell phone: "I can't fucking believe Vonnegut is
dead." Death, or proliferation, of author?)

(A decade later, April 12, 2017, *LA Times* reports: "Calexit backers give up
on ballot measure to secede, Feinstein faces tough crowd in San Francisco")

4.Friday, April 20, 2007
Ulric B. and Evelyn L. Bray Seminar in Political Economy
4:00 pm, 25 Baxter
Networks and Market Makers in the First Emerging Market: Bank of England
Shares, London 1720
Larry Neal
University of Illinois at Urbana-Champaign,
London School of Economics and NBER

(Daily Note: On campus, noticeably heavy police presence after Virginia Tech shootings)

(A decade later, April 20, 2017, *LA Times* reports: "Trump sees cooperation from China in dealing with North Korean 'menace'")

5. Friday, April 27, 2007
William Bennett Munro Memorial Seminar
4:00 pm, Treasure Room, Dabney
Acknowledging the Unthinkable: Returning the Domestic Slave Trade to Its Central Role in the History of the United States
Steven Deyle
Associate Professor, Department of History
University of Houston

(Daily Note: Lingering talk of Imus firing and subsequent apology. How genuine, etc.)

(A decade later, April 27, 2017, *LA Times* reports: "Pentagon is investigating whether Trump's former national security advisor accepted improper foreign payments")

6. Tuesday, May 15, 2007
Ulric B. and Evelyn L. Bray Seminar in Political Economy
4:00 pm, 25 Baxter
Comparative Judicial Politics
Frances Rosenbluth
Department of Political Science
Yale University

(Daily Note: on today's Yahoo page, "TV evangelist Rev Jerry Falwell dies at 73")

(A decade later, May 15, 2017, *LA Times* reports: "A Capitol gathering of Planned Parenthood supporters on Monday had many of the same traits as the January Women's March and other rallies of the Trump era: pink T-shirts and so-called pussy hats, with frequent jeers for the president and the GOP-majority Congress.")

7. Mon., July 9, 2007
Public Lectures on Mars
7:00 p.m., Beckman Auditorium
"A Rover's Eye View of Mars"
Principal Investigator Steve Squyres and
science team members
NASA, Cornell University

(Daily Note: Notes on this exciting talk were particularly difficult to write -- the seating area was darkened so we could take in the images sent to NASA from Mars. During the talk there was mention that this week is a national conference for the Mars results here in Pasadena, California. This talk is not in the Humanities and Social Science Lectures series)

A decade later, July 9, 2017, *LA Times* reports: Fiction Bestsellers:
1. *The Handmaid's Tale* by Margaret Atwood ($15.95)
2. *All the Light We Cannot See* by Anthony Doerr ($17)
3. *Milk and Honey* by Rupi Kaur ($14.99)
4. *Commonwealth* by Ann Patchett ($16.99)
5. *1984* by George Orwell ($9.99)

8. Tuesday, September 25, 2007
Ulric B. and Evelyn L. Bray Seminar
4:00 pm, 25 Baxter
Social Incentives in the Workplace (joint with Oriana Bandiera (LSE) and
Imran Rasul (UCL))
Iwan Barankay
Associate Professor
University of Warwick, Department of Economics

(Daily Note: Driving home from CalTech today, I heard on NPR coverage of the
50th anniversary of the "Little Rock Nine" who integrated Little Rock's
Central high school. One speaker called for students present today to "never
forget from whence they come.")

(A decade later, September 25, 2017, *LA Times* reports: "Cowboys kneel before
national anthem on Monday Night Football")

9. Tuesday, October 2, 2007
Brain, Mind and Society Seminar / Social Science Seminar
4:00 pm, 25 Baxter
Evolving a moral faculty: domain-specificity, neural specialization, and
universality
Marc D. Hauser
Harvard University

(Daily Note: In today's news, LA workers get deal on contract -- six unions
represent about half of city workers. Ends chance of threatened municipal
strike.)

(A decade later, October 2, 2017, *LA Times* reports: "Gov. Jerry Brown,
lawmakers say they 'stand with the people of Nevada' after mass shooting")

10. Wednesday, October 10, 2007
Seminar on History and Philosophy of Science (HPS)
4:00 pm, Einstein Papers Project, 363 S. Hill Ave.
Two Concepts of Scientific Philosophy: Carnap and Reichenbach
Andre Carus
Affiliate Lecturer
University of Cambridge

(Daily Note: In today's news is how "The U.S. State Dept. may phase out use
of Blackwater private security guards in Iraq after review revealed
Blackwater guards protecting U.S. Embassy convoy in Baghdad are accused of
killing 17 civilians.")

(A decade later, October 10, 2017, *LA Times* reports: "Sonoma County officials
on wildfires: 'This is nowhere near over'")

11(A). Tuesday, October 16, 2007
Vicente Fox: Revolution of Hope
The Life, Faith and Dreams of a Mexican President
8:00 pm, Voices of Vision Series
Beckman Auditorium, free

(Daily Note: Today "Putin warns U.S. against attacking Iran" and "Vice
President Dick Cheney and Democratic presidential candidate Barack Obama are
distant cousins.")

(A decade later, October 16, 2017, *LA Times* reports: "The African American
Film Critics Assn. proclaimed 2017 the "Year of the Woman in Cinema," in a
statement Monday announcing the honorees for its ninth annual awards
ceremony.")

11(B). Monday, October 22, 2007
Ulric B. and Evelyn L. Bray Seminar
Noon, 25 Baxter
Schelling Redux: An Evolutionary Dynamic Model of Residential Segregation
William H. Sandholm
Professor of Economics
University of Wisconsin

(Daily Note: Southern California wildfires are zero percent contained)

12. Friday, November 9, 2007
Seminar on History and Philosophy of Science (HPS)
4:00 pm, Treasure Room, Dabney
The Specter of the Telescope: Radical Instrumentalism from Galileo to Hooke
Ofer Gal
University of Sydney

November 9, 2007

(Daily Note: On Spanish-language TV: "Elecciones Controversiales en Bogota,
Columbia" The signs read: "se robaron de las elecionnes de los negros" that
are held at the candidate's bedside.)

November 10, 2007

(Daily Note: Norman Mailer died.)

(A decade later, November 9, 2017, *LA Times* reports: Hillary Clinton helps
Seth Meyers with some jokes he can't tell: "According to a recent article,
Chardonnay is making a comeback," Meyers noted.
"And they said I wouldn't be able to create jobs," quipped Clinton.)

Deborah Meadows is an Emerita faculty member at California State Polytechnic University, Pomona. She lives with her husband in Los Angeles' Arts District/Little Tokyo.

Other Works include:

The Demotion of Pluto: Poems and Plays (BlazeVOX [books], 2017)

Three Plays (BlazeVOX [books], 2015)

Translation, the bass accompaniment: Selected Poems (Shearsman Books, 2013)

Saccade Patterns (BlazeVOX [books], 2011)

How, the means (Mindmade Books, 2010)

Depleted Burden Down (Factory School, 2009)

Goodbye Tissues (Shearsman Press, UK, 2009)

involutia (Shearsman Press, UK, 2007)

The Draped Universe (Belladonna* Books, 2007)

Thin Gloves (Green Integer, 2006)

Growing Still (Tinfish Press, 2005)

Representing Absence (Green Integer, 2004)

Itinerant Men (Krupskaya Press, 2004)

"The 60's and 70's: from *The Theory of Subjectivity in Moby-Dick"* (Tinfish Press, 2003)

Made in the USA
San Bernardino, CA
24 December 2018